THE LITTLE BROWN RICE BOOK

Both convenient and healthy, brown rice can form the basis of a nutritious and appetizing diet.

THE LITTLE BROWN RICE BOOK

by

David Eno

Illustrated by Clive Birch

THORSONS PUBLISHERS LIMITED
Wellingborough, Northamptonshire

This enlarged, revised and reset edition first published
1983

British Library Cataloguing in Publication Data

Eno, David
    The little brown rice book.
    1. Cookery (Rice)   2. Rice, Unpolished
    I. Title
    641.6'3'18   TX809.R5

    ISBN 0-7225-0854-9

Printed and bound in Great Britain

CONTENTS

INTRODUCTION

Convenience foods are becoming increasingly popular, but on investigation prove to have convenience as their only merit. This book is intended to introduce an alternative diet which is both convenient and healthy.

Brown rice is a balanced food containing all the elements necessary to the body. It is possible to live only upon brown rice but for those who have not the stamina of a Zen monk it can at least form the basis of a nutritious diet. It differs from white rice in that it has not been 'polished' to remove the outer skin. It is this skin which contains much of the goodness of the rice grain. In polishing the protein value drops from 9.17% to 8.80%, fat from 2.40% to 0.60%, silicon, magnesium and phosphorous drop 30% to 50% of their former value and vitamins calcium and trace elements are reduced to almost nothing.

Brown rice is nutritious and inexpensive. Most of the recipes which follow are quickly and simply prepared and are therefore easily adapted for one person only.

BUYING AND COOKING BROWN RICE

The best brown rice to buy is the short grain type.

This has less tendency to become a soggy mass and the grains remain separate. It also seems to have a better flavour. Rice is much cheaper when bought in bulk and will keep for up to six months without losing too much of its nutritional value.

Wash the rice in a strainer under the cold tap. The proportions for cooking brown rice are:

> 1 cupful brown rice
> 1½ to 2 cupsful water
> ½ teaspoonful of sea salt

Use cold water and bring to the boil. Reduce heat and simmer gently with a lid on the pan. Do not stir. After 45 minutes the pan should be dry and the rice just beginning to catch the bottom. This harms neither rice nor pan. Allow to stand for a while before using.

Cooked in this way the rice grains remain intact and separate and have a succulent bite to them. Cooked brown rice keeps 4-5 days in a cool place, 5-7 days in a fridge. For convenience cook a large quantity at the beginning of the week.

A wok is invaluable for frying rice and vegetables etc. It is hemispherical and deep enough to fry a large quantity of rice and can be found in Chinese supermarkets and enlightened hardware shops.

BASIC RICE RECIPES

SAKURA RICE

Before cooking brown rice add one tablespoonful of Tamari per cupful of rice and then proceed as normal. Tamari or soy sauce is made by lactic acid fermentation of soya beans, wheat and sea salt and is delicious with brown rice. Avoid imitations made with salt, caramel colouring, etc.

FRIED RICE WITH HERBS

Rice with a difference, for serving with another dish.

1 onion
2 tablespoonsful vegetable oil
2 cupsful brown rice, cooked
2 tablespoonsful fresh herbs, chopped
Seasoning
Tamari

1. Chop the onion finely and fry in the oil until it becomes transparent.

2. Add the rice and heat for 5 minutes, stirring frequently.

3. Turn off the heat and stir in the chopped herbs.

4. Season well and serve with Tamari.

Note: For extra colour add turmeric.

CREOLE RICE

This appetizing but simple way of preparing brown rice is ideal for use with main meals such as curry, quiche, salads, etc.

1 onion, chopped
½ lb (¼ kilo) brown rice
2 tablespoonsful vegetable oil
2 pints (1 litre) water or vegetable stock
Sea salt

1. *Sauté* the chopped onion and rice in the oil until the rice becomes transparent.

2. Add the stock or water, add the salt and bring to the boil. Simmer over a very low heat with a lid on the pan for 20 to 30 minutes. Do not stir whilst cooking

3. After this time the rice should be soft and all the stock will have been absorbed. Serve.

CHINESE VEGETABLE RICE

For a simple snack this plain rice dish can be served by itself or with an omelette. Otherwise it can be used wherever plain cooked rice would be served. It is particularly good with curry.

½ lb (¼ kilo) spring greens
2 oz (50g) butter
4 cupsful brown rice, cooked
1 tablespoonful sea salt

1. Wash the spring greens thoroughly under cold running water and then chop coarsely with a sharp knife.

2. Melt the butter in a saucepan over a medium heat and stir-fry* the greens for 4 minutes adding the salt as cooking proceeds.

3. Add the cooked rice and the water and mix thoroughly. Continue to cook over a low heat with a lid on the pan, preferably using a heat-absorbing mat under the pan.

4. After 15 minutes turn off the heat altogether and leave to stand for a further 10 minutes. By this time the fresh flavour of the greens will have been thoroughly absorbed into the rice and it is ready to serve.

*Stir-frying as practiced in Chinese cooking is a fast and healthy method of cooking vegetables. The cooking time is typically only a minute or two. Vegetables need to be cut into small pieces and should be kept in constant movement while being fried in a small amount of very hot butter or oil. The stirring is usually done by chopsticks or a wooden spoon. The shape of a wok is particularly well suited to stir-frying although it can be done in a normal pan quite successfully.

SPANISH RICE

This makes an attractive side dish for a curry or it can be eaten by itself.

1 large onion
1 clove garlic
2 tablespoonsful vegetable oil
4 oz (100g) mushrooms
½ cupful fresh peas or beans
3 tomatoes
1 tablespoonful parsley, chopped
½ tablespoonful basil, chopped
Sea salt and freshly ground pepper
2 oz (50g) black olives
3 cupsful brown rice, cooked
Tamari

1. Chop the onion finely and fry with the sliced or pulped garlic in a pan with oil.

2. When the onion has softened add the chopped mushrooms and peas or beans and cover the pan. Cook for 10 minutes.

3. Add the chopped tomato, herbs, seasoning, the quartered olives and lastly the rice. Keep turning the mixture until the rice has heated.

4. Serve with Tamari.

MUSHROOMS AND RICE

A quick snack or, with a salad, a complete meal.

½ lb (¼ kilo) mushrooms
2 tablespoonsful vegetable oil
Sprig parsley
3 cloves garlic
4 oz (100g) cooked brown rice
Sea salt
Freshly ground pepper

1. *Sauté* the mushrooms in the oil in a closed pan very slowly until the juices ooze freely.

2. Add the finely chopped parsley and garlic.

3. Stir in the rice and season.

Serves 2

15

TOMATO RICE

1 tablespoonful vegetable oil
1 onion, chopped
1 clove garlic
½ lb (¼ kilo) brown rice
½ lb (¼ kilo) tomatoes
Sea salt
Fresh black pepper
2 cupsful vegetable stock
1 oz (25g) cheese, grated
1 teaspoonful butter
Fresh basil, chopped

1. Heat the oil in a pan and fry the chopped onions and sliced garlic.

2. Stir in the rice and cook until it is transparent, which will take 10 to 15 minutes.

3. Skin the tomatoes by dipping in boiling water for a moment. Chop into small pieces and add to the pan. Season with sea salt and freshly ground pepper.

4. Add the vegetable stock, cover the pan, and simmer for about 20 minutes, when the rice should be cooked and all the stock absorbed.

5. Stir in the cheese, butter and fresh chopped basil and serve straight away.

Serves 4

SALADS

RICE SALADS

Rice can form the basis of many delicious salads. Some specific recipes follow but if you want to create your own try some of the following:

> Cooked beans and other vegetables, chopped or grated carrot, mushroom, onion, spring onions, garlic, tomato, red and green pepper, cucumber, chicory, fennel, celery, watercress, sprouted bean and grains*, nuts, dried fruit, apples, oranges and other fresh fruit, fresh herbs, etc. Decorate with chopped herbs or flower petals, (marigold petals are good). Serve very cool.

As with all salads the dressing is an important element. Although bought dressing can be used the following recipes are for two basic types which are easily made.

* Sprouted beans and grains contain a large proportion of vitamins and are a delicious addition to rice salads. Chinese bean sprouts are sprouted from the mung bean obtainable from wholefood suppliers. Try also red beans, soya beans, black-eyed beans, chick peas, wheat and grains. Soak the beans or grains overnight in a jar with plenty of water. To strain tie a piece of muslin over the

top of the jar and invert. Keep in a warm place, and wash morning and night by adding a little water through the muslin and then straining. When the sprouts are 3 times as long as the seed they are ready — which is 3-5 days.

FRENCH DRESSING

3 tablespoonsful wine vinegar
7 tablespoonsful olive oil
1 tablespoonful honey
½ teaspoonful mustard
Sea salt and freshly ground pepper

Shake all ingredients together in a bottle and sprinkle over your salad.

MAYONNAISE

1 egg yolk
2-4 teaspoonsful wine vinegar or lemon juice
1 cupful vegetable oil
½ teaspoonful clear honey
½ clove of garlic
Sea salt and freshly ground pepper to taste

1. Whisk the egg yolk in a bowl adding a little of the vinegar or lemon juice.

2. Begin adding the oil drop by drop beating rapidly until thickening begins. Continue adding the oil in a slow trickle beating all the time.

3. Add the rest of the ingredients and mix well.

Note: If the oil is added too quickly or if the bowl is not really clean it will separate and, beat as you may, will not thicken. If this happens there is nothing to be done but begin again with a clean bowl and fresh egg yolk adding the separated mixture drop by drop and then the rest of the oil. It always pays to proceed very slowly and patiently in the initial stages.

GREEN RICE SALAD

5 or 6 spring onions
1 medium green pepper
1 bunch watercress
3 sticks celery, chopped
1 apple, peeled, cored and chopped
2 cupsful brown rice, cooked
3 tablespoonsful mayonnaise

1.   Wash the vegetables thoroughly under cold running water and dry in a salad shaker.

2.   Chop the spring onions, green pepper, watercress and celery. Peel, core and chop the apple.

3.   Mix all the ingredients together until the mayonnaise is distributed evenly.

Note: This is particularly good if the mayonnaise has been made with lemon juice.

RICE AND ADUKI BEAN SALAD

Any cooked beans can be substituted in this recipe although aduki beans and brown rice are a particulary good combination.

1 medium onion
2 sticks celery
2 tablespoonsful parsley, chopped
2 cupsful brown rice, cooked
1 cupful aduki beans
2 or 3 drops Tabasco
3 tablespoonsful French dressing or
   mayonnaise
Few slices of cucumber
3 or 4 radishes

1. Chop the onion and celery and mix with the parsley, rice and aduki beans.

2. Mix the Tabasco into the dressing and pour over the salad, stirring well.

3. Decorate with cucumber and radish slices.

23

CURRIES

BEAN CURRY

---

1 onion
4 oz (100g) mushrooms
3 carrots
½ oz (15g) butter
2 cupsful cooked red beans
Curry sauce
3 cupsful brown rice, cooked

1. Cook the finely chopped onion, mushroom and carrots in the butter until they begin to brown.

2. Add the cooked red beans and pour over the curry sauce and simmer very gently for 10-15 minutes.

3. Serve with brown rice.

BASIC CURRY

First the basic curry sauce:

> 4 tablespoonsful vegetable oil
> 2 medium onions
> 2 cloves garlic
> 2 chillies
> 2 cooking apples
> 1 oz (25g) sultanas
> 1 oz (25g) wholemeal flour
> 1-2 tablespoonsful curry powder
> Sea salt and cayenne pepper
> 1½ pints (½ litre) stock or water
> Juice of 1 lime or 1 lemon

1. Heat the oil in a frying pan and add the finely chopped onions and garlic, the sliced chillies and apples, and the sultanas. Cook until the onions begin to brown.

2. Transfer to a saucepan leaving behind as much oil as possible and put aside.

3. Sprinkle the flour and curry powder into the oil. Add a little salt and cayenne pepper and fry until the colour darkens.

4. Pour in the stock little by little at first, stirring constantly until it thickens and then pour over the cooked onion mixture.

5. Simmer with a lid on the pan for 1 hour and then add the juice of 1 lime or lemon.

6. The basic curry sauce can now be served as it is with rice or can be incorporated into one of the following curries. It can also be frozen, which is a useful time-saver.

Note: Side dishes add variety and used with imagination transform a curry into a special meal. Try grated fresh coconut, sliced banana, cucumber in yogurt, finely sliced green peppers, chopped nuts, sliced green apples, nasturtium leaves, cottage cheese with fresh dark cherries. To make an egg curry serve with one boiled egg per person. Alternatively use the following recipe.

EGG CURRY

Curry sauce
4 eggs
3 cupsful brown rice, cooked

1. Whilst the curry sauce is still simmering break the eggs into it and stir until they coagulate into noodle-like strands.

2. Serve with brown rice and dahl.

VEGETABLE CURRY

2 medium onions
1 carrot
2 sticks celery
1 green pepper
Vegetable oil
1 tablespoonful parsley, *chopped*
½ tablespoonful marjoram
3 cupsful brown rice, *cooked*

1. Chop the onions, carrot, celery, and pepper and fry in the oil over a low heat until they soften.

2. Add the curry sauce and cook gently for a further 15 minutes.

3. Add the freshly chopped herbs, and serve with brown rice.

CLIVE BIRCH

MAIN MEALS

RICE FRITTERS

3 tablespoonsful cooked brown rice
4 oz (100g) currants
Grated lemon peel
4 eggs
Raw cane sugar or honey
A little wholemeal flour
Vegetable oil
Grated nutmeg

1. Beat the eggs well in a bowl and spoon in the rice, currants, lemon peel and nutmeg with sugar to taste.

2. Stir in flour to thicken the mixture enough for frying. Cook in hot oil and turn to brown on both sides. If they do not brown quickly add a little more flour.

3. Serve with a squeeze of lemon.

FRIED RICE AND VEGETABLES

The ingredients for this recipe can be varied according to whatever you wish to use up or have available. Use any mixture of finely chopped cooked or uncooked vegetables: carrot, celery, mushrooms, leek, parsnip, pepper and tomato as available. Sprouted grains are an excellent addition and provide an interesting texture. Allow one cupful of cooked rice per person. For a quick and satisfying meal the basic recipe is as follows:

1 onion
2 tablespoonsful vegetable oil
1 cupful vegetables, chopped
2 cupsful brown rice, cooked
1 egg
2 tablespoonsful chopped herbs
Freshly ground pepper
Sea salt
Tamari

1. Fry the finely chopped onion in the oil.

2. Add the vegetables, which may either be pre-cooked or raw, and cook as necessary.

3. When the vegetables are soft add the cooked rice and fry for a few minutes.

4. *Either* break the egg into the mixture and stir

frequently to avoid sticking *or* use it to make an omelette in a separate pan which should then be chopped into strips and added to the rice.

5. Add freshly chopped herbs and season with fresh ground pepper and sea salt.

6. Serve straight away with Tamari.

RICE WITH VEGETABLE STEW

1 onion, chopped
1 clove garlic
2 tablespoonsful vegetable oil
1 green pepper
2 carrots
4 oz (100g) mushrooms
1 lb (½ kilo) tomatoes, skinned
Sea salt and freshly ground pepper
1 teaspoonful cider vinegar
1 teaspoonful yeast extract
1 teaspoonful honey
1 tablespoonful fresh herbs, chopped
2 cupsful brown rice, cooked

1. Fry the chopped onion and garlic in the oil and after a few minutes add the suitably chopped or sliced green pepper, carrots, mushrooms and any other vegetable to hand.

2. Cook for 10 minutes, stirring occasionally and then add the tomatoes and season well.

3. Stir in the cider vinegar, yeast extract, honey and chopped herbs.

4. Cook for a further 15 minutes, or until all the vegetables are soft, then adjust seasoning before serving with brown rice.

Serves 2

SAVOURY RICE FRITTERS

2 eggs
4 oz (100g) brown rice, pre-cooked
2 oz (50g) Cheddar cheese, grated
1 onion, chopped
1 tablespoonful 81% self-raising
   wholemeal flour
2 tablespoonsful milk
1 level teaspoonful yeast extract
Sea salt
Freshly ground pepper
2 tablespoonsful oil

1. Separate the egg yolks from the whites. Mix
    the rice, grated cheese, onion, flour, egg
    yolks, milk and yeast extract to form a thick
    batter. Season with sea salt and freshly
    ground pepper.

2. Beat the egg whites until stiff then fold into
    the batter.

3. Heat the oil in a frying pan and drop in
    dollops of the batter, a tablespoonful at a
    time, frying both sides until golden brown.
    Keep warm in a low oven until all the fritters
    are cooked.

4. Serve with salad, or with steamed vegetables
    and gravy.

STUFFED MARROW

1 cupful brown rice
1 tablespoonful yeast extract
1 medium marrow
2 oz (50g) butter
1 large onion
2 eggs, hard-boiled
2 large tomatoes
2 tablespoonsful parsley, chopped
Sea salt
Freshly ground pepper

To garnish:
1 large tomato
1 lemon

1. Set the rice to cook in a covered pan with 2 cupsful of water and the yeast extract.

2. Remove the ends of the marrow and cut into slices 2½ in (5cm) wide. Scoop out the seeds with a spoon. Cook the marrow in a large pan of boiling salted water for 20 minutes or until tender and then drain well.

3. Melt the butter in the pan and *sauté* the finely sliced onion.

4. When the onion is soft stir in the cooked rice, the sliced, hard-boiled eggs and the peeled

and chopped tomatoes and the chopped parsley.

5. Season with salt and pepper.

6. Place the cooked marrow on a pre-heated serving platter and fill each slice with the rice mixture. Garnish with more parsley and a slice each of tomato and lemon on top. Serve straight away.

RICE CARROT CASSEROLE

2 cupsful cooked brown rice
2 cupsful shredded carrots
2 eggs, beaten
½ onion, chopped finely
2 teaspoonsful yeast extract
1 cupful milk
1 cupful grated cheese
Tarragon

1. Blend all the ingredients togther in a mixing bowl and turn into an oiled casserole.

2. Set in a pan of hot water and bake at 350°F/190°C (Gas Mark 4) for 45 minutes.

Serves 4

RICE AND TOMATO BAKE

2 tablespoonsful vegetable oil
1 onion, chopped
1 clove garlic
½ lb (¼ kilo) brown rice
2 pints (1 litre) water or vegetable stock
1 oz (25g) butter
1 lb (½ kilo) tomatoes
Freshly ground pepper
2 tablespoonsful parsley, chopped
2 tablespoonsful cheese, grated

1. Heat the oil and *sauté* the chopped onion, garlic and rice for about 10 minutes until the rice becomes transparent.

2. Add the stock or water and bring to the boil.

3. Simmer over a very low heat with a lid on the pan for 20 to 30 minutes. Do not stir whilst cooking.

3. After this time the rice should be soft and all the stock will have been absorbed.

4. Butter an oven-proof dish and make alternate layers of rice and sliced tomatoes sprinkling each layer with a little pepper and chopped parsley.

5. Top with a layer of grated cheese and bake

for 15 minutes at 450°F/230°C (Gas Mark 8).

Serves 4

STUFFED PEPPERS

4 large peppers
1 onion
1 clove garlic
2 tablespoonsful oil
2 cupsful brown rice
½ cupful vegetable stock or water
2 teaspoonsful yeast extract
2 tablespoonsful tomato purée
1 tablespoonful chopped parsley

1. Select large perfect peppers. Wash and slice off the tops and remove all the seeds.

2. To prepare the stuffing, chop and fry the onion and garlic lightly in the oil. Add the cooked rice and pour in a little stock or water. Stir in the yeast extract and tomato *purée*. Season well adding the chopped parsley.

3. Stuff the peppers and replace the tops. Place in an oven dish with a little water to prevent sticking. Bake for 45 minutes at 350°F/180°C (Gas Mark 4).

Note: Excellent with garlic mayonnaise. Cabbages, tomatoes, globe artichokes can be stuffed in the same manner.

RISOTTO

2 tablespoonsful oil
1 onion, chopped
1 clove garlic
1 cupful uncooked brown rice
2 cupsful vegetable stock
1 tablespoonful yeast extract
½ tablespoonful chopped rosemary
3 tablespoonsful chopped parsley
½ cupful grated cheese
Seasoning

1. *Sauté* the onion and garlic in oil over a low heat. When soft add the rice and cook for a further 5 minutes, stirring constantly. The rice should turn a golden colour.

2. Dissolve the yeast extract in the stock and sprinkle in the herbs, freshly chopped if available, and pour half the stock over the rice.

3. Continue to cook over a low heat adding more stock as it is absorbed. The rice should be tender in 30 minutes.

4. Add ¼ cupful of cheese and when it has melted remove from the heat.

5. Top with the rest of the cheese and serve.

Serves 4

RISOTTO MILANESE

2 oz (50g) butter
2 tablespoonsful olive oil
½ lb (¼ kilo) brown rice
1 onion, chopped
1 clove garlic, pulped
¾ pint (400ml) vegetable stock
Pinch of saffron
1 small glass white wine
4 oz (100g) mushrooms
3 oz (75g) Parmesan cheese, grated
1 tablespoonful parsley, chopped

1. Take a heavy iron casserole or skillet with a lid and melt the butter and oil over a low heat.

2. Stir in the rice and keeping the pan covered cook for 10 minutes. Add the finely chopped onion and garlic and cook for 5 minutes longer.

3. Add ½ pint of the vegetable stock and continue cooking slowly until the stock is absorbed.

4. While the rice is cooking add the saffron to the wine and leave to steep for a few minutes.

5. Add the remainder of the stock, the wine and

saffron, and the chopped mushrooms to the rice and stir together gently.

6. Cover the pan and allow to cook a little longer until all the liquid is again absorbed.

7. Stir in the cheese and turn into a pre-heated serving dish.

8. Garnish with slices of tomato and chopped parsley and serve.

PILAFF

½ lb (¼ kilo) brown rice
3 tablespoonsful vegetable oil
1 pint (½ litre) stock or water
½ lb (¼ kilo) tomatoes
1 onion
Seasoning

1. Wash and rinse the rice. Drain thoroughly and cook for 5 minutes in oil over a gentle heat.

2. Pour in the heated stock and simmer for 15-20 minutes. By this time the liquid should be absorbed and the rice dry and soft.

3. Thinly slice the tomato and stew with the onions for 5-7 minutes. Gently stir this into the rice and serve.

Serves 4

RICE CROQUETTES

1 large leek
2 tablespoonsful vegetable oil
4 oz (100g) grated cheese
2 cupsful brown rice, cooked
2 tablespoonsful wholemeal flour
Sea salt
Freshly ground pepper
1 egg
¼ cupful milk
Wholemeal breadcrumbs

1. Chop the leek finely and fry in the vegetable oil until soft.

2. Mix the leeks with the grated cheese, rice, flour and seasoning, adding a little milk to bind if necessary. Form into croquettes and dust with flour.

3. Beat the egg with a little milk and coat the croquettes, then dip in breadcrumbs and fry in oil until crisp.

4. Serve with a salad or cooked vegetables and top with chutney or pickle.

Although there are a number of vegetarian gravy powders on the market I have not found any of these as good as this simple recipe which produces excellent results in just a few minutes.

4 tablespoonsful vegetable oil
2 tablespoonsful 81% wholemeal flour
1 pint (½ litre) cold water
2 teaspoonsful tomato purée
1 tablespoonful yeast extract

1. Heat the oil in a pan and stir in the flour to make a roux. Leave to cook for a few minutes, but do not allow to brown.

2. Stir in the water little by little and when it is all added bring to the boil.

3. Stir in the tomato *purée* and yeast extract and leave to simmer for a few minutes. Strain if necessary and keep hot until needed.

SNACKS

FORTIFIED PORRIDGE

Excellent for a cold winter morning

1 cupful rolled oats
3 cupsful milk or water
1 tablespoonful raisins
1 teaspoonful sea salt
1 cupful cooked brown rice
1 apple, chopped
1 tablespoonful hazelnuts, chopped
Honey to taste

1. Add the raisins to the milk and bring to the boil.

2. Stir in the oats, salt, chopped apple and nuts. Cook for 4-5 minutes over a gentle heat.

3. Add the brown rice and cook for a further 2 minutes. Sweeten to taste with honey.

4. Serve with milk or cream.

Serves 3

RICE SOUP WITH VEGETABLES

This is a really good way of using up cooked left-over rice and vegetables. Rice fried with vegetables or any selection of rice and vegetables cooked separately can be used.

> 1 medium onion
> 1-2 cloves garlic
> 1 tablespoonful vegetable oil
> 2 cupsful of mixed rice and vegetables
> 2 pints (1 litre) vegetable stock
> Sea salt and freshly ground pepper
> Chilli powder
> 2 tablespoonsful parsley, chopped

1. Fry the chopped onion and a clove of pulped or sliced garlic in a little vegetable oil using a large pan.

2. Add the rice and vegetables which have been thoroughly liquidized with the vegetable stock. Season with sea salt and freshly ground pepper.

3. Add the chopped parsley and the smallest pinch of chilli powder, but exercise great caution here. The very tip of a pointed knife is the best measure to use, as it is easy to ruin your soup with too much.

4. Heat up the soup again and taste to see if any further seasoning is required.

KITCHEREE

5 oz (125g) brown rice
5 oz (125g) red lentils
1 pint (½ litre) water
1 teaspoonful sea salt
1 oz (15g) butter
1½ teaspoonsful garam masala*
3 tomatoes
1 green pepper

1. Wash the rice and lentils together in a sieve under cold running water.

2. Add one pint of water and cook in a covered pan for 35 to 45 minutes when all the water will be absorbed and the rice cooked.

3. Stir in the salt and butter and garam masala and serve hot, garnished with slices of tomato and green pepper.

*Garam masala is used in many Indian curry dishes and is now widely available. However it is easy to mix and grind your own using a coffee grinder. Take 2 oz (50g) of black peppercorns, 2 oz (50g) of coriander seeds, 1½ oz (35g) of black caraway seeds, ½ oz (15g) of cloves, ½ oz (15g) of cinnamon, and about 20 cardamons, which should have their outer skin removed and grind together. Like all ground spices the mixure soon loses its flavour, so make in small batches and keep in an airtight container.

RICE OMELETTE

1 cupful brown rice
2 mushrooms
1 onion
2 tablespoonsful vegetable oil
3 eggs
Herbs and seasoning
Tamari

1. Fry the rice, mushrooms and onion in the oil.

2. Beat the eggs in a bowl and have another pan ready with 1 teaspoonful of very hot oil. Pour in the eggs and as the bottom layer hardens keep lifting to allow the liquid to flow beneath.

3. When the egg is nearly set sprinkle with ground pepper and sea salt and add the filling with a dash of tamari.

4. Fold the omelette and serve.

Note: This is especially good with spinach tossed in butter, garlic and lemon juice.

Serves 2

CHEESE AND ONION QUICHE

I include this recipe, not because it contains rice, but because rice is such a natural accompaniment for it. This is a general recipe for a cheese and onion quiche — some variations follow.

3 oz (75g) vegetable margarine
6 oz (150g) wholemeal flour
Sea salt
Ice-cold water
1 onion
4 oz (100g) cheese, grated
3 eggs
½ pint (¼ litre) milk
1 tablespoonful wholemeal flour
2 tablespoonsful fresh herbs, chopped
Sea salt and freshly ground pepper

1. To make the pastry rub the fat into flour and add salt to taste. When of breadcrumb consistency add a little ice cold water and knead lightly.

2. Roll out and line a 9 in (20cm) greased flan tin. For cheese pastry add 1 cupful grated cheese at the breadcrumb stage. Prick the pastry with a fork and bake blind for 10 minutes at 350°F/180°C (Gas Mark 4).

3. Chop and fry the onion until tender and spread in the flan case. Cover with the grated cheese.

4. Beat the eggs, milk, flour, herbs, and seasoning, and pour into the flan case. Decorate with slices of tomato before baking. Place in the oven and cook for 30 minutes at 375°F/190°C (Gas Mark 5) after which the egg should be set and the top should be golden brown.

5. Serve with sakura rice or rice and mushrooms with a salad.

Variations:
Mushroom Quiche — Add 4 oz (100g) of mushrooms to the above. Chop and fry the mushrooms with the onion.
Leek and Tomato Quiche — Chop 2 medium leeks into short lengths and boil or steam for 10 minutes. With or without the cheese add the leeks with the onion and when the flan is ready to go into the oven top with slices of fresh tomato.
Herb Quiche — Leave out the cheese, replace the milk with single cream, and add 2 extra tablespoonsful of fresh chopped herbs.
Bean Quiche — Add 1 cupful of cooked beans to the onions in the flan case.

RICE POTATO CAKES

1 lb (½ kilo) boiled potatoes
Sea salt
Freshly ground pepper
1 egg
2 oz (50g) cheese, grated
1 cupful brown rice, cooked
1 tablespoonful milk
2 teaspoonsful wholemeal flour
2 oz (50g) wholemeal breadcrumbs
2 tablespoonsful vegetable oil

1. Mash the potatoes or rub through a sieve and season with the sea salt and pepper.

2. Beat the egg in a cup and stir half into the potato.

3. Mix in the grated cheese, cooked rice and milk.

4. Form into cakes and dust with the flour. Leave to stand for at least an hour.

5. Dip in beaten egg and then breadcrumbs. Fry to crisp golden brown in the oil.

RICE PUDDING

1 egg
3 cupsful cooked brown rice
1 cupful milk
Pinch sea salt
1 tablespoonful honey
1 tablespoonful raisins or sultanas
1 teaspoonful cinnamon
Nutmeg, freshly grated

1. Beat the egg and mix with the rice and honey.

2. Add the other ingredients except for the nutmeg and bake for 30 minutes at 350°F/180°C (Gas Mark 4).

3. Sprinkle on the nutmeg and serve.

INDEX